KRISTALLNACHT

BY STEPHANIE FITZGERALD

COMPASS POINT BOOKS
a capstone imprint

Compass Point Books are published by Capstone,
1710 Roe Crest Drive, North Mankato, Minnesota 56003
www.mycapstone.com

Editorial Credits
Sarah Bennett, Jaclyn Jaycox, Angela Kaelberer, Kelli Lageson,
Kathy McColley, Catherine Neitge, and Svetlana Zhurkin

Photo Credits
Alamy: John Frost Newspapers, 12, 84, Martin Shields, 52, 101 (left); Getty
Images: Bettmann, 61, 88, Corbis Historical/Hulton-Deutsch Collection, 45,
Galerie Bilderwelt, 76, Hulton Archive/Keystone, 63, Hulton Archive/Picture
Post/Gerti Deutsch, 80, Keystone, 59, 71; Granger, NYC - All rights reserved:
11; Library of Congress, 19, 51; National Archives and Records Administration,
14, 41; National Archives/Press Association, 103 (top right); National
Archives/U.S. Army, 17; Newscom: akg-images, 22, 48, 65, 93, 96, akg-
images/Bildarchiv Pisarek, 2, 46, 73, 83, 102 (left), EPA/STR, 6, 101 (right),
Everett Collection, 28, Jewish Chronicle Heritage Images, 42, Picture History,
26, Pictures from History, 8, 56, 87, cover, St. Petersburg Times PSG/JOSEF
FRIEDRICH COEPPICUS, 79, World History Archive, 95, ZB/picture alliance/
Agentur Voller Ernst, 98; Shutterstock: Everett Historical, 20, 25, 30, 33, 35,
38, 54, 66, 90, 102 (right), ilolab, throughout (background), Roman Nerud,
37, 100, U.S. Army/US Army Military History Institute, 103 (bottom left),
XNR Productions, 47, 81

Library of Congress Cataloging-in-Publication Data
Names: Fitzgerald, Stephanie, author.
Title: Kristallnacht / by Stephanie Fitzgerald.
Description: North Mankato, Minnesota : Capstone, [2018] | Series:
Eyewitness to World War II | Age 10–12, grade 4–6. | Includes bibliographical
references and index.
Identifiers: LCCN 2017009739 | ISBN 9780756555832 (library binding)
| ISBN 9780756555870 (paperback) | ISBN 9780756555917 (ebook pdf)
Subjects: LCSH: Kristallnacht, 1938—Juvenile literature. | Holocaust, Jewish
(1939-1945)—Juvenile literature. | Jews—Persecutions—Germany— Juvenile
literature.
Classification: LCC DS134.255 .F579 2018+ | DDC 940.53/1842—dc23
LC record available at https://lccn.loc.gov/2017009739

Printed and bound in the USA.
010368F17

CONTENTS

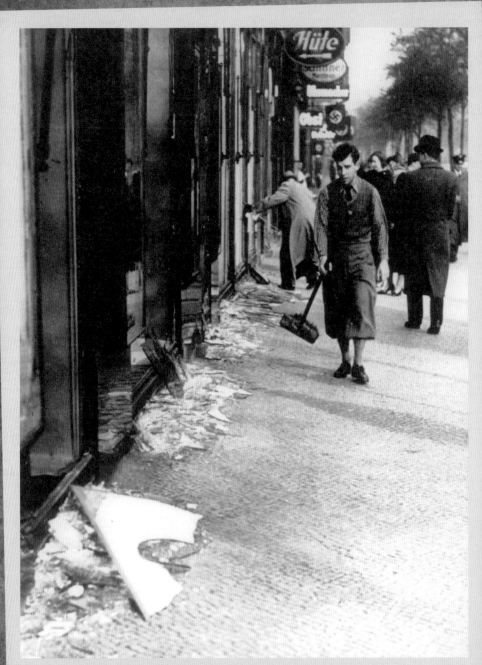

On the morning of November 10, 1938, Jewish shop owners cleaned up what was left of their businesses. Storm troopers destroyed the windows of nearly 8,000 Jewish shops during what became known as the Night of Broken Glass.

CHAPTER ONE

NIGHT OF DESTRUCTION

Crash! Thirteen-year-old Arnold Fleischmann awoke with a start very early in the morning of November 10, 1938. Arnold lived in the town of Bayreuth, Germany, but he was staying with the Bloom family in the nearby city of Nuremberg while he studied for his bar mitzvah. This important religious ceremony for a Jewish boy was to take place on November 12.

Arnold remembers German soldiers in brown shirts walking into his bedroom carrying daggers. "We pretended to be asleep even though they turned the lights on. They didn't bother us. They walked back out. They smashed all the kitchen dishes and china closets, turned over the furniture and made sure just about everything was broken."

SA storm troopers stood guard outside a shattered Jewish-owned business in Vienna, Austria.

Arnold didn't know it then, but he was in the middle of a huge pogrom—an attack on Jewish people—that was going on in Germany and Austria. Known as Kristallnacht, the Night of Broken Glass, the pogrom was meant to frighten Jews into leaving their home countries. Chancellor Adolf Hitler and the National Socialist German Workers' Party, known as the Nazi Party, had controlled Germany since 1933. Hitler and the Nazis falsely blamed German Jews for many of the country's problems and had been making life in the country difficult for them since taking power. Beginning the night of November 9, Nazi leaders encouraged their private army, known as the Sturmabteilungen (SA), to destroy Jewish businesses, homes, and synagogues. The streets and sidewalks were covered with shattered window glass. The SA storm troopers and others beat and even killed Jewish men.

After smashing up nearly everything of value in the house, the soldiers at the Bloom residence found several Torahs, which are religious scrolls. After

THE NIGHT OF BROKEN GLASS

Kristallnacht means "night of crystal" in German and is often called the Night of Broken Glass. It got its name from the shattered glass that lined the streets after Jewish homes, businesses, and synagogues were attacked. At the time, Germany didn't manufacture enough plate glass for its country's windows. It imported glass from other countries. It took a Belgian company six months to replace all the broken windows.

setting fire to them, they arrested Mr. Bloom and took him away. Arnold knew he had to find out what was happening to his own family. He walked to a public telephone and called his family in Bayreuth. He learned that his father, grandfather, and uncle had all been arrested earlier that morning.

Arnold boarded a train and reached his home in
Bayreuth around 9 a.m. His grandfather and uncle were
quickly released, but his father, a leader of the town's
Jewish community, was being held in the city jail.
Arnold was able to take some food to his father at the jail.
About a week later, his father was released.

Arnold's planned bar mitzvah never happened.
SA troops had burned Jewish synagogues and schools
during Kristallnacht. "There was this total collapse
of what it was like to be a Jew in Germany," he said.
"After Kristallnacht I was afraid. I had seen enough
of the cruelty of the Nazis and the so-called innocent
bystanders who had seen these things and done nothing."

Arnold was right. During Kristallnacht, police
officers and firefighters stood by while the SA and others
destroyed and burned Jewish property, only making an
effort to keep the flames from spreading to non-Jewish
areas. Some townspeople threw rocks through store
windows, while others hurried past the violence with
their faces turned away. A few brave people warned
their Jewish neighbors or even hid them in their homes.

Firefighters worked to prevent fires from spreading to nearby homes, but did nothing to save a synagogue from burning in the aftermath of Kristallnacht.

But they weren't in the majority. As British news reporter Hugh Carleton Green observed, "Racial hatred and hysteria seemed to have taken complete hold of otherwise decent people. I saw fashionably dressed women clapping their hands and screaming with glee,

On November, 11, 1938, *The Daily Telegraph* in London reported on attacks of Jewish properties across Germany.

while respectable middle-class mothers held up their babies to see the 'fun.'"

During Kristallnacht, nearly 8,000 Jewish-owned businesses and homes were damaged and looted. Hundreds of synagogues were leveled, most by fire, and nearly 100 Jews were killed. Another 30,000 were sent to concentration camps. News of the huge pogrom was printed in newspapers throughout Europe and the United States. But there were little or no efforts made to help the Austrian and German Jews.

Kristallnacht sent a message to the world that the Nazis wanted the Jews out of Germany and its territories and would do whatever they needed to accomplish that goal. The lack of reaction from the rest of the world also sent a message to the Nazis. Kristallnacht was likely just the beginning.

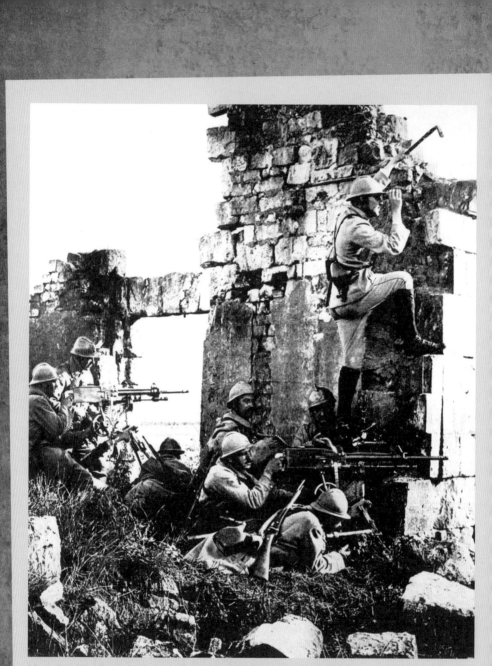

More than 65 million soldiers from 30 countries fought in World War I.

CHAPTER TWO

GERMANY
IN RUINS

How did something as violent as Kristallnacht
happen? Its roots can be traced to the anger and
despair the German people felt following World War I.

World War I began on June 28, 1914, when a Serbian
man, Gavrilo Princip, assassinated Austrian Archduke
Franz Ferdinand and his wife as they rode in a car
through Sarajevo, capital city of Bosnia and Herzegovina.
Princip and other Serbians were angry about Austria-
Hungary's control of Bosnia and Herzegovina. On July 28
Austria-Hungary declared war on Serbia. Russia came
to Serbia's defense, and on August 1 Germany declared
war on Russia. By the end of August 1914, Great Britain,
France, Belgium, and Japan were involved in the fighting.
Germany, Austria-Hungary, the Ottoman Empire, and

Bulgaria formed an alliance called the Central Powers. Their opponents were the Allied Powers of Great Britain, Russia, and France, along with several other countries. In 1917 the United States also joined the Allies.

By the time it ended on November 11, 1918, World War I was one of the bloodiest and most expensive wars ever, with nearly 9 million soldiers and 13 million civilians killed and more than 20 million people seriously wounded. The war cost the countries involved $185 billion. The Allied nations shouldered the biggest burden, about $125 billion.

After the war the Allies blamed Germany for starting the war. The Allies wanted to make sure that Germany would never be able to start another war. As part of the Treaty of Versailles, which was signed June 28, 1919, Germany lost much of its territory in Europe. They also were told to pay reparations of $33 billion to the Allied countries for the money they spent fighting the war. Germany was left in ruins and its people were furious. They blamed not just the Allies for their situation. Many Germans also blamed their Jewish neighbors.

The signing of the Treaty of Versailles brought World War I to an end.

Many people in Germany and other European countries were anti-Semitic. They hated Jews and wanted to blame them for their problems. These Germans thought that the German Jews had betrayed German soldiers by

A STAB IN THE BACK

When Germany surrendered in November 1918, many Germans called this "forced" surrender the *Dolchstoss*, meaning "stab in the back." Many believed that German Jews had forced the surrender. But that wasn't true. German army leaders asked the government to seek terms of surrender because the soldiers weren't able to continue fighting. But German military leaders and certain politicians deliberately hid this information from the German people. They claimed that German Jews and members of various socialist and liberal political parties had pressured the government to surrender. They referred to them as the "November criminals."

pushing the government to surrender and sign the Treaty of Versailles.

Anger over the outcome of the war led to new political parties, such as the Nazi Party, which formed in 1919 as the German Workers' Party. Adolf Hitler, who had served as a corporal in the German army during World War I, joined the party soon after it formed. By 1921 Hitler was leading the party, which was known as the National Socialist German Workers' Party.

Despair over the conditions of the Treaty of Versailles wasn't the only factor that helped the Nazis gain power in Germany.

During the 1920s Germany experienced a period of major inflation. Prices for goods rose to extremely high amounts as the German currency, the mark, became worth very little. "My father was a lawyer," remembers Walter Levy, a German-born consultant, "and he had taken out an insurance policy in 1903, and every month he had made the payments faithfully. It was a 20-year policy, and when it came due, he cashed it in and bought a single loaf of bread." Prices increased rapidly. For example, a person would order a cup of coffee costing 5,000 marks at a café. By the time the waiter brought the bill, the price had increased to 7,000 marks. People used their nearly worthless cash to buy

German marks became so worthless, people burned the paper money as fuel to heat their homes and cook their meals.

19

things they didn't want or need and then bartered them for what they did need.

As life in Germany became more desperate, Hitler's popularity grew. Many Germans liked Hitler's promises to not only restore Germany's world position but also to raise the country to new heights of power. He pledged to revive the economy, rebuild the army, and regain the territories that Germany lost after World War I, plus expand into new ones. Hitler believed that the Germans and other Europeans of Nordic descent formed a "master race" that was superior to all other ethnic groups. He referred to these people as Aryans—ideally, people

with fair skin, blond hair, and blue eyes. He believed Aryans were responsible for all the advances in world history, and that Germany would become great again only if the country rid itself of non-Aryans, especially Jews. He also wanted to expel all other ethnic minorities and people who were physically or mentally disabled. How exactly he planned to do this wasn't known to many people at the time—perhaps not even to Hitler himself. But as the Nazi Party grew in power and

An enthusiastic crowd saluted Adolf Hitler as he went by in a parade.

JEWS IN GERMANY

About 500,000 Jews lived in Germany in 1933. About one-fifth of them weren't German citizens. They were immigrants from Eastern Europe, mainly Poland. Whether they were citizens or not, most Jews were loyal members of German society. Many were poor, but there was also a strong Jewish middle class. Many Jewish people owned or worked in small businesses, such as clothing or furniture shops, or were doctors and lawyers.

Hitler's bitter anti-Semitism was the keystone of his plan for Germany. He believed that Jewish people held too much power and were responsible for almost everything bad that happened in the world. Though Hitler's ideas must have made them uncomfortable, few Jewish Germans realized until too late the depth of his hatred for Jewish people or the lengths to which he would go to force them out of Germany.

A Jewish bookshop in 1920s Berlin

strength, that all changed. Soon Hitler's plans for non-Aryan people were terrifyingly clear.

Hitler was determined to isolate and harass the Jews in Germany to the point where they would want to leave the country. At this time in history, the Nazis were not focused on the mass murder of Jews—they wanted to make Germany *Judenfrei*, meaning "Jew free," or *Judenrein*, meaning "pure of Jews."

A FATEFUL ANNIVERSARY

Kristallnacht occurred on the 15th anniversary of a failed Nazi attempt to take over the government, called the Beer Hall Putsch. Adolf Hitler and about 20 other Nazis walked into a Munich beer hall on November 8, 1923, where a political meeting was taking place. Gustav von Kahr, the state commissioner general of Bavaria, led the meeting. Hitler fired a gun toward the ceiling and called for a new national government, which he would lead. The crowd cheered him, but after Hitler left the hall, Kahr alerted the military to be on the watch for the Nazis.

The next morning Hitler found out that his coup hadn't played out the way he planned. But he decided to make a final stand. At 11 a.m. Hitler and about 2,000 Nazis marched to the center of Munich. During a standoff with police, someone fired a shot, which killed a police sergeant. The police opened fire on the demonstrators. Four policemen and 16 Nazis were killed, and many others were wounded.

Hitler fled and hid in a friend's home for two days before he was found and arrested. He was sentenced to five years in prison. While in prison, Hitler wrote the first volume of *Mein Kampf* (*My Struggle*), which told of his anti-Semitic beliefs

A crowd gathered to hear a speaker at the Beer Hall Putsch in Munich.

and outlined his goals for Germany. Hitler was released on parole on December 20, 1924, after only nine months in jail. Two months later he again was leading the Nazi Party. But he had no intention of making the mistake of an attempted coup again. Hitler was determined to be elected Germany's leader, which would allow him to legally implement his plans to bring Germany back to its former glory.

Huge crowds greeted Adolf Hitler, who would rapidly rise to power in Germany's government.

CHAPTER THREE

HITLER'S RISE TO POWER

After Adolf Hitler's release from prison in 1924, the Nazi Party began to rebuild. Hitler's strength as an orator, combined with Germans' frustration over the crumbling national economy, helped persuade more people to support the party. But the Nazis didn't have much success running for office until 1930, when they received 18 percent of the total vote. With that victory, the Nazis went from the smallest party in Germany to the second largest.

In July 1932 Nazi candidates were elected to 230 of the 608 seats in the German Parliament, the Reichstag. The Reichstag was dissolved in September, and new elections were held in November. In that election, the Nazis lost some of their seats. Hitler ran for president, but lost to incumbent president Paul von Hindenburg. The following January, though, Hindenburg appointed Hitler to the position of chancellor, which was the head of the democratic government.

President Paul von Hindenburg (center) appointed Adolf Hitler as chancellor in hopes that doing so would keep the Nazi Party under control.

The next month the Reichstag building burned, and the Nazis blamed members of the Communist Party, who opposed the Nazis. Hitler used the incident to seize even more power from Hindenburg. On March 23 members of the Reichstag passed the Enabling Act, which effectively ended democratic government in Germany and gave Hitler absolute power.

Hitler wasted no time exercising his new powers. On April 1, 1933, the Nazis organized a nationwide boycott of Jewish-owned businesses. Lists of Jewish shops were distributed in every town. The Jewish symbol, the Star of David, was painted on the fronts of Jewish-owned shops, as were

PRESIDENT VS. CHANCELLOR

After World War I, the president was the head of the German government. Paul von Hindenburg held the elected position from 1925 until 1934. Under the German constitution, the president had the power to appoint the chancellor, who reported to both the president and the Reichstag. Today, though, the power of the positions is reversed. The office of president is largely a ceremonial position. The German chancellor is the head of the government, running the country with the aid of the parliament.

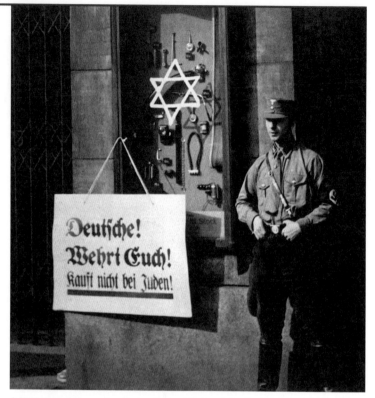

A Nazi storm trooper stood in front a Jewish store in Berlin, Germany, beside a sign reading "Germans, defend yourselves, do not buy from Jews."

Nazi swastikas and the word Jude, the German word for Jew. Anti-Jewish graffiti also appeared on the storefronts. People were encouraged to report any Germans who ignored the boycott, and SA troops stood outside Jewish businesses to threaten anyone who tried to enter.

But the boycott wasn't a success. Most Germans didn't support it, and some even went out of their way to visit Jewish-owned businesses. The government canceled it after the first day. But later that month, Hitler outlawed non-Aryans from working in government jobs. In parts of Germany, kosher butchering, the Jewish way of preparing animals for slaughter, was also now illegal.

KOSHER BUTCHERING

Orthodox Jews strictly follow the laws of the Jewish holy book, the Torah. They adhere to traditional practices, which include eating only foods that are kosher. Hitler's law against kosher butchering made them face some difficult choices.

Schlomo Wahrmann's father, a kosher butcher, ignored the law and kept providing kosher meat for the Jews of Leipzig. Wahrmann later wrote about this experience:

"Often, my younger sister would carry the [koshering knife] to the chicken market because we were confident the Gestapo [secret police] would not apprehend such a young girl. Nonetheless, my mother remained tense."

Other Orthodox Jews chose to live without meat. Jewish newspapers in Germany printed vegetarian recipes, and, in 1935, Germany's League of Jewish Women published a vegetarian cookbook.

Another law limited the number of non-Aryan students allowed to attend public schools and universities, allegedly to reduce crowded classes.

President Hindenburg died August 2, 1934. With Hindenburg gone, Hitler had no limits on his quest for power. He combined the positions of president and chancellor and named himself führer—the absolute ruler of Germany. The democratic constitution was no longer in effect. Right away, Hitler went after his political enemies. Storm troopers arrested and imprisoned or killed hundreds of people whom Hitler believed threatened his leadership.

Hitler continued to work toward a Germany that was Judenfrei. "Jews Not Wanted" signs started to appear in hotels, theaters, sports stadiums, and restaurants. Similar signs were posted on the roads leading into villages and towns.

The Reichstag passed the Nuremberg Laws on September 15, 1935. They defined Jews not as people who followed the Jewish religion but as those who had Jewish ancestry, such as three Jewish grandparents.

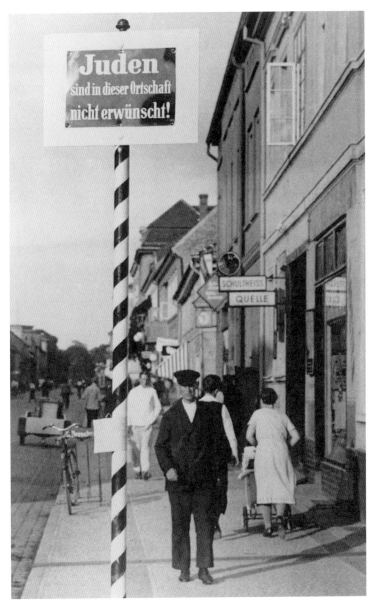

Signs reading "Jews Not Wanted" were posted all around Germany.

The laws stripped German Jews of their citizenship and forbade them from dating or marrying non-Jewish Germans or flying the German flag. Life was difficult for German Jews, and by 1938, more than one-quarter of them had left the country, many for the United States or European countries. Some who wanted to leave were unable to, either because of cost or quotas. But many stayed, believing that German citizens would soon come to their senses and oust Hitler from power. For many of them, it was an error in judgment that would prove fatal.

NIGHT OF THE LONG KNIVES

Sometimes even Hitler's friends weren't safe from his anger and paranoia. He became convinced that the SA was planning to seize his power. On the night of June 30, 1934, Hitler ordered the executions of his old friend, SA head Ernst Röhm, and dozens of Röhm's officers. The purge became known as the Night of the Long Knives, from a German saying about revenge.

A FRIGHTENING SYMBOL

Symbols became an important part of the Nazi persecution of Jewish people. Hitler selected the swastika to represent the Nazi Party in 1920. The name of the hooked cross comes from the Sanskrit word *svastika*, meaning "good fortune" or "well-being." For ancient people it may have represented the sun moving through the sky. It's still used as a sacred symbol by religions such as Buddhism and Hinduism. Hitler may have first seen the symbol as a child when he attended a school in a monastery in Lambach, Austria. The swastika was on the Nazi flag and also decorated military uniforms and vehicles.

WHO WAS ADOLF HITLER?

Although Adolf Hitler became a world leader, his early life was marked by failure. Hitler was born April 20, 1889, in Braunau am Inn, Austria, to Alois and Klara Hitler. Alois had two older children from an earlier marriage. When Adolf was 4 years old, his brother Edmund was born, followed by sister Paula two years later. Edmund died of the measles when Adolf was 10.

Adolf did well in grade school, but struggled once he entered high school. He loved to draw and wanted to attend an arts high school. His father wanted him to work in a government job and sent him instead to a technical high school. Adolf hated the school and spent much of his time misbehaving and playing pranks. One teacher said that Adolf "reacted with ill-concealed hostility to advice or reproof; at the same time, he demanded of his fellow pupils their unqualified subservience, fancying himself in the role of leader." Alois Hitler died when his son was 13 and wasn't around to prevent Adolf from quitting school at age 16.

After leaving school, Hitler spent his time reading, drawing, painting, and visiting art galleries and museums. In October 1907, at age 18, he applied to the Vienna Academy of Fine Arts. When he was rejected, it was a huge blow to him, as was his mother's death two months later. Soon after, he returned to Vienna and again applied to the

Academy of Fine Arts. Again, he was rejected. He ran out of money but didn't try very hard to find a job. By the winter of 1909, he was living in a homeless shelter. He did odd jobs and also found some work as an artist, selling postcard-sized paintings. He still read extensively, focusing on politics, philosophy, and German history. The books helped form the ideas he later put into practice as head of the Nazi Party and Germany.

Hitler moved to Munich in 1913, volunteering for the German army when World War I began in 1914. He was wounded in action and received five medals, but only rose to the rank of corporal—the second-lowest rank in the army. After the war Hitler remained in the army and worked as an undercover agent.

In September 1919 he received an assignment to investigate the new German Workers' political party. He was impressed with the party's ideas, which were similar to his own. He joined the party, which would later become the Nazi Party. Before long he was giving fiery speeches about Germany's problems and how to solve them. Hundreds of people came to party meetings just to listen to him. In 1921 he became the party's leader—a position he would keep for the rest of his life.

Thousands of German soldiers participated in the annual Nuremberg Rally. The rallies of the Nazi Party showcased Germany's military power to the rest of the world.

CHAPTER FOUR

THOUSAND-YEAR REICH

The official name for the Nazi government was the Third Reich. Reich means "empire" in German. Germans used the term to refer to periods in their country's history. During the First Reich, Germany was part of the Holy Roman Empire, from about 962 until 1806. The Second Reich was the German Empire, which began in 1871 with the unification of Germany and lasted until the collapse of the country in 1918 after World War I. Hitler referred to the Third Reich as the Thousand-Year Reich because he predicted the Nazis would rule Germany for 1,000 years.

Breaking the rules of the Treaty of Versailles, Hitler formed a new army, navy, and air force. German soldiers moved into the Rhineland, an area in western Germany near the borders of Belgium, Luxembourg, and France, on March 7, 1936. According to the Treaty of Versailles, the area was to be demilitarized. No German military forces were permitted to be stationed in the Rhineland. But no countries tried to stop them. The countries were still recovering from World War I. Rather than confront Hitler, British and French leaders tried to work with him. They thought that if they gave Hitler what he wanted, he would be content and stop demanding more. But the opposite was true. The more he got away with, the more confident Hitler became. He decided that Austria was next on the list for a German takeover.

Hitler met with Austrian chancellor Kurt von Schuschnigg in February 1938 and demanded more power for the Nazi Party in Austria. Schuschnigg refused and was eventually forced to resign by members of the party. Arthur Seyss-Inquart, the leader of the Austrian Nazi Party, took over. Seyss-Inquart invited the German army to invade Austria, which it did on March 12. The result was the Anschluss, a union between Germany and Austria.

Enthusiastic Austrians welcomed the German takeover in March 1938.

About 200,000 Jewish people were living in Austria at the time. This was nearly equal to the total number of Jews who had been forced to emigrate from Germany in the early 1930s. On March 11, knowing the Germans would soon occupy their country, Austrian Nazis in Vienna staged an attack on their Jewish neighbors.

Any Jewish person caught on the streets was beaten or humiliated. Some were forced to clean army toilets or

Jewish people were forced to clean the streets of Vienna after the Anschluss. Onlookers stood by while they were made to perform the tasks.

scrub slogans supporting former chancellor Schuschnigg off the sidewalks. Jewish businesses were looted and destroyed, and Jewish people were arrested or fired from their jobs. The Austrian police did nothing to stop the Nazi attackers. In many cases, they merely stood by and watched.

DISCRIMINATION AGAINST JEWISH PEOPLE

Discriminatory laws and policies weren't the only things that made life hard for Jewish people in Germany. The rude treatment they received from their non-Jewish neighbors also made day-to-day life difficult.

In public, some Germans would point out people they thought were Jewish by commenting on their looks or an imagined smell. But they often were mistaken.

Historian Marion Kaplan wrote about one such incident: "In one case, a woman remarked upon three children seated across from her in a train compartment. She admired the two "Aryan" types and denigrated [belittled] the darker girl. The father of the two finally told her that the two blonds had a Jewish mother and the darker one was "Aryan.""

The Austrians' actions against the Jewish people impressed the German Nazis. The *Schwarze Korps*, a weekly Nazi newspaper, reported: "They have managed to do overnight what we have failed to do up to this day in the slow-moving, ponderous north. In Austria, a boycott of the Jews does not need organizing—the people themselves have instituted it with honest joy."

CZECHOSLOVAKIA'S FATE

In September 1938 Czechoslovakia became a victim of Europe's hopes to keep Hitler happy. Hitler wanted the Sudetenland to be under German control. The region, with its large German population, had become part of Czechoslovakia after World War I. When the leaders of Germany, Great Britain, France, and Italy met in Munich to discuss the situation, the head of Czechoslovakia was not invited. At the meeting, the leaders signed an agreement that transferred the Sudetenland to Germany. When Czechoslovakian President Eduard Beneš protested the decision, he was told by Great Britain's leadership that it was not willing to go to war with Germany over the Sudetenland.

The graffiti on Jewish shops in Austria warned the owners that if they cleaned up the hateful slogans, they would be sent to a concentration camp.

A number of Jewish Austrians saw no way out and committed suicide. A report in *The New York Times* said that as many as 170 Jewish people were taking their own lives every day. Thousands more left Austria for neighboring countries, some traveling as far as Great Britain and the United States. But all countries

JEWISH IMMIGRATION

Between 1933 and 1939, about 95,000 German and Austrian Jews legally immigrated to the United States. Approximately another 60,000 Jews settled in Palestine in the Middle East, which at the time was ruled by Great Britain as part of the peace agreement made after World War I. In the 1920s many Jewish people had immigrated to the area to create a Jewish state. In the late 1930s, German Jews saw Palestine as the perfect place for them to escape the Nazis' tyranny.

Thousands of Jewish people left Nazi Germany after the Nuremberg Race Laws of 1935. The laws took away German citizenship rights from Jews, making them "subjects of the state."

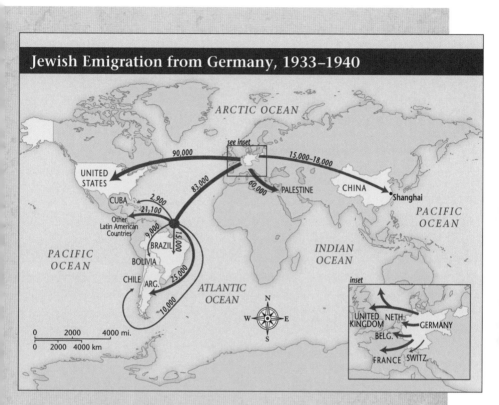

Jewish Emigration from Germany, 1933–1940

In Palestine, they believed they would truly be welcomed. But it was the British government, not the Jewish people living there, who decided which people would be allowed into Palestine. The British government set severe limits on the region's immigrant quotas.

As fewer European nations agreed to accept Jewish refugees, thousands of German, Austrian, and Polish Jews traveled to Shanghai, China. The city was one of the few places in the world that had no visa requirements.

had quotas limiting the number of immigrants they would allow to enter their borders. Countries such as the United States made their immigration policies as difficult as possible for Jewish refugees. Officials would demand documents they knew would be impossible for the immigrants to get or would simply reject their

The first Kindertransport arrived in Harwich, England, on December 2, 1938, carrying nearly 200 Jewish children. The British government agreed to let children from Germany enter the country and stay temporarily until the "crisis was over."

A FAILED ATTEMPT AT HELP

U.S. President Franklin Roosevelt was concerned about what was happening to the Jews in Austria and Germany. In March 1938 he invited representatives from around the world to a conference in Evian-les-Bains, France. He asked them to form a committee to help political refugees emigrate from Austria and Germany.

The Evian Conference took place in July. Representatives from 32 countries attended. Although Roosevelt had called for the conference, he didn't attend or send a high-ranking government official. Instead, he sent a friend, businessman Myron Taylor.

Of all the countries gathered at the conference, only the Dominican Republic offered to increase its immigration quotas. Other countries, including the United States and Great Britain, lowered their quotas. Like many people around the world, many Americans were anti-Semitic.

The United States was also in the middle of the Great Depression. American politicians and citizens were afraid that unemployed Jewish immigrants would compete with Americans for the few jobs available. The failure of the Evian Conference encouraged Hitler to keep persecuting the Jews. He realized that although other countries condemned what he was doing, they weren't willing to step in to stop him.

applications. This frustrated Nazi leaders in Germany, who had planned to make life so difficult for Jewish people that they would choose to immigrate to other countries. But no other country was willing to take many of them.

Nazi leaders realized they had to take more drastic action against the Jewish population. In a series of new laws and decrees, the government increased its efforts to identify and isolate its Jewish residents. On April 26, 1938, Hermann Göring, the Nazi economic minister, said that all Jewish holdings valued at more than 5,000 reichsmarks (approximately $1,200) would have to be registered. This rule allowed the Nazis to keep track of and use Jewish wealth in Germany.

Beginning in June 1938, more than 2,000 Jewish and other people were arrested on charges of "race pollution." Simply living among the Aryan population was considered a crime. The people who were arrested were taken to one of the four concentration camps in Germany—Dachau, Buchenwald, Lichtenburg, or Sachsenhausen.

A FAMOUS IMMIGRANT

The Nazis' desire to rid themselves of all Jewish people robbed them of some of the most brilliant minds of the time. Among those was the noted physicist Albert Einstein.

Einstein was born in 1879 to a Jewish family in Ulm, Germany. As a young man, he developed the mass/energy equivalence formula, $E=mc2$. His theory of general relativity, published in 1916, helped people understand how space, time, light, and gravity work together. He won the Nobel Prize for physics in 1921.

By 1933 Einstein was alarmed by the rise of the Nazi Party in Germany. He renounced his German citizenship and moved to the United States, saying, "I shall live in a land where political freedom, tolerance, and equality of all citizens reign." He settled in New Jersey and became a U.S. citizen in 1940. He continued his scientific research and discoveries until his death in 1955.

A policy took effect in August requiring Jewish men with names not recognized as Jewish to use the middle name "Israel" and women to use the middle name "Sarah." According to both the Hebrew and Christian Bibles, Israel and Sarah were ancestors of the Jews. The names would allow the Nazis to easily identify anyone having Jewish ancestry. In October Jewish passports were no longer valid. New passports were stamped with the letter "J" and Jews were forced to carry special identity cards.

A Jewish passport from 1939 Nazi Germany was stamped with a large "J" on the left side to identify the holder, Max Reinhold, as Jewish.

At a meeting on October 14, 1938, Göring gave the signal that new, drastic measures were about to begin. "The Reich must eradicate doubtful elements from the population," he told his colleagues. "Namely, the last remaining Jews."

The Nazis just needed the right opportunity. Less than a month later, that opportunity came to them through the actions of a 17-year-old Polish Jew who had grown up in Germany. His name was Herschel Grynszpan.

A WORLDWIDE DEPRESSION

The Great Depression of the 1930s was unique—it was an economic downturn that affected the whole world rather than just one country. Nations tried to boost their own industries by attaching high tariffs on foreign goods. But the policy to tax imports slowed foreign trade, which made the Depression drag on for years. It is estimated that 30 million people worldwide were without jobs by 1932. In countries such as Germany, Italy, and Japan, the instability was a leading cause of the rise of fascism—a form of dictatorship.

CONCENTRATION CAMPS

Early concentration camps were built as detention and work camps for political prisoners, people whom the Nazis considered enemies, and people who broke the laws of the Reich.

The first such camp opened in the town of Dachau in southern Germany in 1933. The Sachsenhausen camp opened in 1936, followed by Buchenwald in 1937. Although individual prisoners were often murdered, these camps were not death camps designed for mass extermination of prisoners. The Nazis' six killing centers, Auschwitz-Birkenau, Belzec, Chelmno, Majdanek, Sobibor, and Treblinka, were built later.

In the concentration camps, the inmates worked for 14 to 16 hours a day, often breaking and hauling stones for building projects. They were forced to stand in line in the hot sun, sometimes for 15 hours at a time. During this time the prisoners didn't receive any food or water, and they couldn't get out of line to use the bathroom. At Buchenwald and Sachsenhausen, the prisoners worked to enlarge the camps. At Dachau, they were forced to sew the Star of David on thousands of striped uniforms for prisoners to wear.

Two prisoners at Buchenwald concentration camp supported a comrade, since fainting was often an excuse to kill inmates who could no longer work.

Herschel Grynszpan wanted to avenge brutal Nazi oppression.

CHAPTER FIVE

A SHOOTING IN PARIS

Herschel Grynszpan was born in 1921 in Germany. His parents, Zindel and Rivka, were Jews who had emigrated from Poland 10 years before Herschel was born. He attended a yeshiva—Jewish school—in Frankfurt as a teenager. At age 15 he left the yeshiva and returned to his parents' home. He wanted to immigrate to Palestine, but wasn't allowed to do so because of his age.

Herschel's parents were concerned about what was happening to Jews in Germany and wanted their son to be safe. They sent him to live with his uncle and aunt, Abraham and Chawa Grynszpan, in Paris, France. Herschel, who had a Polish passport, was allowed to travel to Belgium to visit another uncle. From there, he crossed into France illegally in September 1936.

Because he was in France illegally, Herschel wasn't able to work or attend school. He spent his days in the coffeehouses and movie theaters in Paris. His Polish passport had expired in January 1938, and French authorities informed him in August that he had to leave the country. Afraid to return to Germany, he stayed illegally in France, under constant fear of being discovered. He kept up with what was happening to the Jews in Germany by reading the *Pariser Haint*, a Yiddish-language newspaper published in Paris.

Herschel was alarmed to read a story on October 31, 1938, reporting that 12,000 Polish Jews had been deported from Germany in the last few days of October. On November 3 he received a postcard from his sister, Berta. As Herschel read the postcard, his worst fears were realized. His sister wrote: "You undoubtedly heard of our great misfortune. I will describe to you what happened. On Thursday evening rumors circulated that all Polish Jews had been expelled from a city. But we didn't believe it. On Thursday evening at 9 o'clock a Sipo [security policeman] came to us and informed us that we had to go to Police Headquarters. Almost our

Thousands of Polish Jews were expelled from Germany, but Polish authorities refused to take them. They lived in Zbaszyn on the Polish-German border for many weeks in a refugee camp.

entire quarter was already there. A police van brought all of us right away to the Rusthaus. All were brought there. We were not told what it was all about, but we saw that everything was finished for us. Each of us had an extradition order pressed into his hand, and one had to leave Germany before the 29th. They didn't permit us to return home anymore. I asked to be allowed to go home to get at least a few things. I went, accompanied by a Sipo, and packed the necessary clothes in a suitcase. And that is all I saved. We don't have a Pfennig [cent]. More next time."

A few days later, Herschel received another postcard from his sister. The family had been taken by train to the village of Zbaszyn, near Poland's border with Germany. They were stuck there while the Polish government decided if they could take the refugees. Berta wrote, "We are very poorly fed. We sleep on straw sacks. We have received blankets. But, believe me . . . we won't be able to stand this much longer." She closed the message by begging her brother to send money.

Jews deported from Germany cooked in buckets outside their living quarters in Zbaszyn, Poland, where they lived in stables.

On November 6 Herschel asked his uncle Abraham for money to send to his family. Abraham refused, saying he had little money to spare and even if he did, there was no address to send it to. Herschel was angry at his answer, and the two got into a shouting match. Finally, Abraham told Herschel that if he didn't like living under his rules, he could leave. Furious, Herschel stormed out of the apartment with the little money he had. Before he left, though, Abraham threw 200 francs at him. Instead of attempting to send the money to his family, Herschel came up with a different idea about how to spend it. He used a little of the money to buy food and rent a room at a small hotel, where he spent the night. By that time, Abraham had calmed down and went out to look for his nephew. He never found him.

At 8:35 a.m. the next morning, Monday, November 7, Herschel walked into *A La Fine Lame* (At the Sharp Blade), a store that sold guns and ammunition, just as it was opening. "I want to buy a revolver," he told the owner.

Herschel paid 210 francs for a 6.35 mm revolver and another 35 francs for a box of ammunition. The owner, Monsieur Carpe, showed him how to load and fire the gun. Herschel was supposed to fill out a declaration form for his gun and hand it in to the police. He never made it to the police station, though. Instead he went to a café. In the café's bathroom, he unwrapped the gun and loaded five cartridges in its chambers. He then walked out of the café and down the street.

By 9:30 a.m., Herschel had reached his destination—the German Embassy. He politely asked to see the German ambassador and was told he was not in. At that same moment, a man walked past Herschel on his way out of the embassy. It was the ambassador, Count Johannes von Welczeck. He had heard Herschel ask for him but didn't want to delay his morning walk, so he didn't stop. That decision likely saved his life.

Once inside the embassy, Herschel told porter Henri Nagorka that he had an important document and

German diplomat Ernst vom Rath

needed to see someone who knew German secrets. Nagorka offered to take the document, but Herschel insisted that he needed to deliver it personally. Nagorka then took Herschel to see Ernst vom Rath, the only official who was on duty that early in the morning. Vom Rath told Herschel to sit down, but Herschel remained standing.

When vom Rath asked to see Herschel's document, the young man reached into the inside pocket of his

jacket and pulled out his gun. "You are a *sale boche*
[French for a "dirty Kraut"] and in the name of 12,000
persecuted Jews, here is the document!" he screamed.

Herschel fired five shots at vom Rath at point-blank
range, hitting him twice. But to Herschel's surprise,
the diplomat didn't fall dead to the ground. Vom Rath
staggered to his feet as he called for help. Herschel stood
there, staring at his victim. He made no attempt to reload
the gun and shoot vom Rath again.

Nagorka ran to the room after he heard the shots and
vom Rath's calls for help. More help arrived as a doctor
and a French police officer named Autret were called to
the scene. Instead of trying to escape, Herschel just sat
passively in a chair.

On the way to the police station, Herschel spoke to
Autret. "I've just shot a man in his office," he said. "I do
not regret it. I did it to avenge my parents, who are living
in misery in Germany."

As soon as Hitler learned of the shooting, he ordered
his personal physician to Paris to take care of vom Rath.

A FINAL MESSAGE

At the hotel where Herschel Grynszpan spent the night before the shooting, he wrote a note to Abraham and Chawa Grynszpan on the back of a postcard with a photo of himself that he kept in his wallet. He started the note in Hebrew with the words "with God's help." Then he continued in German: "My dear relatives, I couldn't do otherwise. God must forgive me. My heart bleeds when I think of our tragedy and that of the 12,000 Jews. I have to protest in such a way that the whole world hears my protest, and this I intend to do. I beg your forgiveness."

A handwritten postcard by Grynszpan to his aunt and uncle indirectly hinted at the assassination to come.

The Nazis sponsored an elaborate funeral of Ernst vom Rath, who was assassinated by Herschel Grynszpan.

CHAPTER SIX

NIGHT OF TERROR

News of the assassination attempt was first reported on November 8, just as members of the Nazi Party were gathering in Munich to commemorate the anniversary of the Beer Hall Putsch. Joseph Goebbels riled up the crowd by speaking about Herschel Grynszpan's attack.

The assassination gave the Nazis the excuse they needed to stage a widespread assault on Jewish people in Germany and Austria. Nazi leaders later claimed that Germans were outraged about vom Rath's shooting and took it out on the country's Jewish people. But this story was just Nazi propaganda. Nazi leaders at the highest level ordered the pogroms that took place on November 9 and the following day.

The Nazi propaganda ministry ordered all of Germany's newspaper editors to make sure the story of the assassination dominated the front page of every paper. An editorial headlined "The Criminals" in the Nazi newspaper *Völkischer Beobachter* read: "It is clear that the German people will draw their own conclusion from this new deed. It is an impossible situation that within our frontiers hundreds of thousands of Jews should control our shopping streets, places of entertainment, and as 'foreign' landlords pocket the money of German tenants, while their racial comrades outside call for war against Germany and shoot down German officials."

Hitler learned about Ernst vom Rath's death in an afternoon phone call but pretended to learn about it as he ate dinner in Munich's old town hall chamber that night. In a "drama carefully

NO VOICE

While the Nazi newspapers expressed outrage over the assassination and called for revenge, German Jews remained publicly silent. All Jewish newspapers and magazines were banned, and the Jewish community had no voice to comment on the event.

staged by Hitler and Goebbels," witnesses recalled
that after he received a telegram, Hitler pushed away
his plate and spoke "agitatedly" to Goebbels, who
was sitting next to him. Goebbels later said that they
discussed demonstrations against Jews that had recently
taken place around Germany. He said Hitler told him
that although the party should not organize similar
demonstrations, it should not stop any that might occur
"spontaneously." Other people who were there said they
heard Hitler say that "the SA should be allowed to have
a fling."

Hitler then got up and left the hall. This was
unusual. Hitler usually gave the closing speech at these
gatherings. But this was all part of Hitler's and Goebbels'
plan. Now no matter what was said or happened after he
left, Hitler could always claim that he had never given
any specific orders. Instead, Goebbels gave the closing
remarks, saying, in part: "I have news for you here
tonight, to demonstrate what happens to a good German
when he drops his guard for one moment. Ernst vom
Rath was a good German, a loyal servant of the Reich,

working for the good of our people in our embassy in Paris. Shall I tell you what happened to him? He was shot down! In the course of his duty, he went, unarmed and unsuspecting, to speak to a visitor at the embassy, and had two bullets pumped into him. He is now dead. Do I need to tell you the race of the dirty swine who perpetrated this foul deed? A Jew! Tonight he lies in jail in Paris, claiming that he acted on his own, that he had no instigators of this awful deed behind him. But we know better, don't we? Comrades, we cannot allow this attack by international Jewry to go unchallenged. . . I ask you to listen to me, and together we must plan what is to be our answer to Jewish murder and the threat of international Jewry to our glorious German Reich!"

After hearing Goebbels' speech, Nazi leaders believed that Herschel Grynszpan wasn't the only one who was to blame for vom Rath's death; it was all Jews—and they all needed to be punished. A message went out from the headquarters of the German secret police, the Gestapo, to all local police bureaus, alerting them that the SA would be carrying out demonstrations against

Joseph Goebbels was a high-ranking Nazi and close friend of Hitler, who named him minister of public enlightenment and propaganda.

Jews that night. The police were told not to interfere, except to prevent looting. They were also told to expect the arrests of 20,000 to 30,000 Jews, particularly those who were wealthy. Police were also told that although synagogues and community centers could be burned to the ground, businesses and homes were to remain intact. The Nazis wanted the Jews out, but they wanted to save their property so the Nazis could confiscate it after the Jewish owners were forced out.

By midnight on November 9, attacks on Jewish businesses, homes, and synagogues were well underway in the Third Reich. Mobs roamed the streets of German cities and towns, shouting anti-Semitic slogans.

In Munich, mobs torched the first synagogue at midnight. Firefighters tried to control the flames as they began to spread to a nearby Jewish school. But the SA officers cut their hoses and added gasoline to the fire. The firefighters had no choice but to watch both buildings burn.

In Berlin the pogrom didn't start until 2 a.m. on November 10, to give police time to get ready. Police identified Jewish property that would be destroyed and set up roadblocks to keep traffic away from those

A synagogue in Berlin was just one of many synagogues destroyed during Kristallnacht.

areas. They also wanted firefighters standing by to make sure that fires didn't spread from synagogues to nearby homes or businesses. By dawn, nine of the city's 12 synagogues had been burned.

In Cologne the police handed out axes and weapons to the SA and other members of the crowd. They also supplied a list of names and addresses of Jewish property to be destroyed. The police didn't want to risk any Aryan property accidentally being targeted. Seventeen Jewish shops in the city center were destroyed.

In Nuremberg the SA destroyed nearly all Jewish property before turning on the Jews themselves. Nine Jewish people were murdered. Some were beaten to death, one was thrown from the window of his house, and another was thrown down his own staircase repeatedly until he died. Ten more Jewish people were reported to have committed suicide.

If Jewish-owned property was left in Nuremberg after Kristallnacht, the Nazis stole it. Many Jewish people were forced to sign over their properties for a fraction of what they were worth. A synagogue worth more than 100,000 reichsmarks ($24,000) was sold for 100 reichsmarks ($24). Nazi officials told Jews that they must agree to sell or they would be killed. By

November 14 most of the Jewish property in Nuremberg was in the hands of the local Nazi Party.

THOSE WHO DARED SPEAK OUT

Some non-Jewish Germans had the courage to speak out against the Nazi violence during Kristallnacht. Pastor Julius Von Jan led a Lutheran congregation in the town of Oberlenningen in the Swabia region of Germany. The Sunday after Kristallnacht, he preached to his congregation about the evils of the pogrom: "Houses of worship have been burned down with impunity [without fear of punishment]. Men who served our nation and have done their duty have been thrown into concentration camps because they belong to a different race. Our nation's infamy is bound to bring about divine punishment."

Von Jan was quickly punished for his words. A Nazi mob beat him and threw him onto the roof of a shed. They then destroyed his house. Von Jan was arrested and tried. He served five months of a 16-month prison sentence. In 1943 he was drafted into the army. After surviving the war, he returned to his church. He died in 1964.

The attacks were especially violent in Austria and the Sudetenland, perhaps because SA members there were eager to show their loyalty to Germany. Freddie Knoller, who was a boy in Vienna, Austria, at the time, later recalled the terror that gripped him and his family

Jewish women in Austria were forced to sit in public with cardboard signs stating, "I have been excluded from the national community."

that night: "Somewhere around 11 that night, we heard a noise in our courtyard, and looking down we saw the Storm Troopers talking to our caretaker. He took them into the building. My mother became quite hysterical: 'What are they going to do? Where are they going? Are they coming up to us?' My father turned off the lights so that the apartment was in darkness. Suddenly we heard a woman's shrill voice, a screaming voice, and we heard the glass of a window breaking. We heard a thud in the courtyard. We looked down and saw a body lying there. We didn't know who it was until the woman, Mrs. Epstein from the first floor, came running into the courtyard, screaming and going to her husband's body."

As the looting and destruction wound down on November 10, the arrests began. Jewish men of all ages were rounded up and marched through the streets as their German neighbors shouted insults at them.

Fourteen-year-old Esther Ascher went out into the streets of her hometown of Breslau that morning. She remembers, "The streets were deserted except for SS men, marching with a Jewish male between them."

Esther walked through the streets and saw destruction of property everywhere. Soon she had seen enough and turned around to go home. "The picture was the same: SS men leading Jews who followed them as innocent lambs. . . . From that point on life changed for me. I had but one goal, to leave Germany."

During the week following Kristallnacht, more than 30,000 Jewish men were arrested and sent to the concentration camps at Buchenwald, Dachau, and Sachsenhausen. The arrests marked a change in Nazi policy. Before Kristallnacht, Jewish people had to have committed some type of offense against the Reich to be sent to the camps. The men arrested and sent to the camps after Kristallnacht were guilty of only one thing. They were Jewish.

The Nazis didn't plan to keep the Jewish people arrested after Kristallnacht in the camps very long. Their imprisonment was intended to encourage them to leave

Germany. The prisoners were told that they would be released if they were ready to leave the country immediately. Gestapo officials also warned the prisoners that if they told anyone about what happened at the camps, they would immediately be arrested and returned to them.

Nazi storm troopers led Jewish men from the town of Baden-Baden, Germany, to be transported to the Dachau concentration camp in 1938.

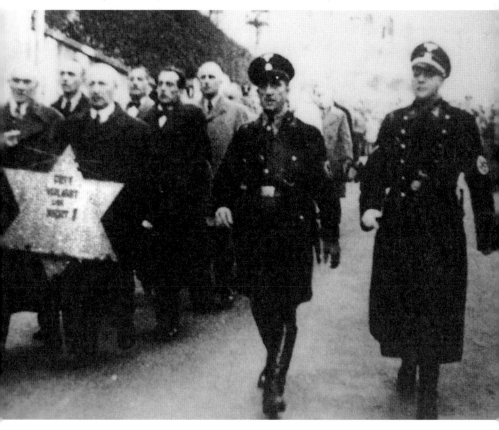

THE KINDERTRANSPORT

After Kristallnacht, the British Committee for the Jews of Germany appealed to members of Parliament to allow German immigrants into the country. After much debate, it was decided that an unspecified number of children younger than 17 would be allowed into Britain. The program was known as the Kindertransport. The first transport left Germany less than one month after Kristallnacht. About 10,000 children made the trip. The last transport left Germany on September 1, 1939. The last transport left the Netherlands on May 14, 1940, when that nation surrendered to Germany. In Britain, some children were sent to orphanages or group homes, some were taken in by foster families, and others worked on farms. Most of the children never saw their families again.

Refugee children stayed at a holiday camp at Dovercourt Bay near Harwich after arriving in Britain in December 1938. The children were part of the Kindertransport operation.

Kristallnacht, November 9–10, 1938

LATVIA
SWEDEN
Baltic Sea
LITHUANIA
North Sea
DENMARK
DANZIG
Königsberg
Danzig
EAST PRUSSIA (GER.)
U.S.S.R.
Kiel
Lübeck
NETHERLANDS
Hamburg
Stettin
Bremen
GERMANY
Hannover
Berlin
Beckum
POLAND
Düsseldorf
Cologne
Leipzig
Dresden
BELGIUM
Bonn
Breslau
Frankfurt
LUXEMBOURG
Nuremburg
Sudetenland
CZECHOSLOVAKIA
FRANCE
Freiburg
Munich
Linz
Vienna
Salzburg
HUNGARY
ROMANIA
LIECHTENSTEIN
SWITZERLAND
AUSTRIA
YUGOSLAVIA
ITALY

0   75   150 mi.
0   75   150 km

- Cities where synagogues were destroyed
Former borders, 1933
Land added to Germany, 1938

As a result of the Kristallnacht pogrom on the night of November 9 and the following day, nearly 8,000 Jewish-owned stores, warehouses, and houses were damaged or destroyed. Nearly 300 synagogues were burned or otherwise demolished. As many as 2,500 Jews—including men, women, and children of all ages—died as a result of Kristallnacht, mostly in concentration camps.

SANCTIONS AGAINST JEWS

The emboldened Nazis published new decrees against Jews on November 14, 1938. Jews could no longer attend concerts, movies, and other public performances. The next day, German Education Minister Bernhard Rust issued an order that banned all Jewish children from German schools. "After the ruthless murder in Paris, no German teacher can any longer be asked to give lessons to Jewish schoolchildren," he said. "It goes without saying that it is intolerable for German pupils to sit in the same classroom with Jews." Jewish children were allowed to attend only schools run by the Jewish communities.

On December 3 the Decree on the Utilization of Jewish Property forced all Jewish businesses to be sold to non-Jews, usually for prices far below their market value. Starting December 6, Jewish people were forbidden to walk or drive in certain places. In Berlin the ban covered all public recreational facilities, including theaters, concert halls, museums, parks, and swimming pools. Any Jewish person caught in one of the banned places could be fined 150 reichsmarks ($36) or spend six weeks in prison.

Jewish people were also forbidden to walk on many of the streets in Berlin. Jewish people who

Jewish schools were closed in 1942 as part of the extermination plan for European Jews.

lived on the banned streets were told to leave and find somewhere else to live. Hotel owners asked for a decree that would ban Jews from their inns. Soon other cities and towns enacted similar restrictions.

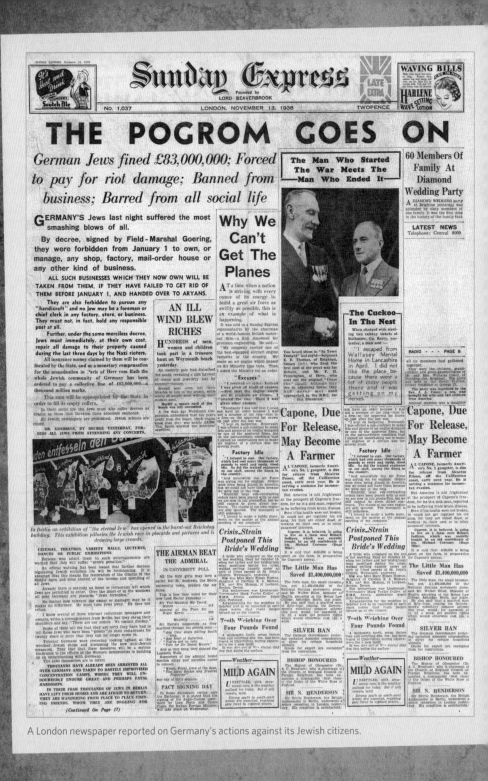

A London newspaper reported on Germany's actions against its Jewish citizens.

CHAPTER SEVEN

AFTERMATH OF KRISTALLNACHT

Newspapers worldwide published stories about what happened in Germany and Austria on November 9 and 10. People in other countries were horrified and demanded an explanation.

Adolf Hitler and Joseph Goebbels responded to the worldwide newspaper stories by holding a press conference for foreign correspondents in Berlin on November 11. Goebbels told the reporters that German citizens were responsible for the violence because of their anger about Ernst vom Rath's assassination. But the reporters weren't satisfied with Goebbels' explanation. They pressured him to tell the truth.

For once, Goebbels appeared to be taken aback. He insisted that if Jews around the world continued to spread exaggerated stories about the event—as he claimed they were doing in American newspapers—"they would be digging the graves of the Jews in Germany."

The day after the press conference, Goebbels was back to business as usual. He believed that the Nazis had gotten away with Kristallnacht and was confident that no matter what they did to the Jews, there would be no consequences. The Nazis also hoped that being candid about their plans to get rid of the Jews would encourage other nations to find a place for Jewish refugees.

But despite the world's outrage over Kristallnacht, other European governments didn't condemn the Nazi government's actions. Many countries were unwilling to upset international trade, risk involvement in another war, or create policy problems at home. British Prime Minister Neville Chamberlain still refused to speak out against Hitler, even though members of the press and the British Parliament pressured him to do so. The subject was never even brought up in the French government.

Neville Chamberlain served as prime minister of the United Kingdom from May 1937 to May 1940.

Even Jewish people living outside of Germany didn't have a strong response. Three days after Kristallnacht, representatives of the General Jewish Council met in New York City to discuss a response to the pogrom. According to a report in *The Jewish Week*, the members of the council were worried about anti-Semitism in the United States and decided "that there should be no parades, public demonstrations or protests by Jews."

Only one world leader publicly condemned the Nazi government and its actions—U.S. President Franklin D. Roosevelt. On November 15, he said, "The news of the last few days from Germany has deeply shocked public

Franklin D. Roosevelt was the first and only world leader to speak out against the Nazi government after Kristallnacht.

opinion in the United States. Such news from any part of the world would inevitably produce a similar profound reaction among American people in every part of the nation. I myself could scarcely believe that such things could occur in a twentieth-century civilization."

Roosevelt then brought the American ambassador back home from Berlin—something that had not happened since World War I. But the situation for Jews in Germany didn't improve.

It's impossible to say whether anything—except another world war—could have made Hitler give up his plans for Germany. But perhaps if the rest of the world had acted sooner, the horrible things that happened to European Jews could have been avoided.

It took World War II for countries to band together to stop Hitler. The war began September 1, 1939, when Germany invaded Poland. Great Britain and France declared war on Germany on September 3. A year later Germany entered into an alliance with Italy and Japan, when leaders of the three nations signed the Tripartite Pact. The three countries, together with Bulgaria, Croatia,

Hungary, Romania, Slovakia, and Yugoslavia, formed the Axis powers. The Soviet Union was also a German ally for a time, since Hitler and Soviet Premier Joseph Stalin had signed a nonaggression plan in August 1939.

German soldiers invaded Poland in September 1939. It was the beginning of World War II in Europe.

By June 1941 the Nazi empire covered most of Europe as the German army marched across the continent, meeting little resistance. Denmark, Norway, Belgium, the Netherlands, France, and Luxembourg all fell under

German control. But Hitler then made a fatal error by invading his former ally, the Soviet Union, on June 22, 1941. In December 1941 the United States entered the war after Japan bombed the U.S. naval base at Pearl Harbor, Hawaii. The United States joined Britain, the Soviet Union, and China as the Allied forces.

At the same time the Germans were expanding their empire, they were increasing the number of "undesirables" within that empire. Forcing Jewish people to emigrate or placing them in concentration camps no longer satisfied them. The Nazis came up with a new plan known as the Final Solution. The policy was coordinated at the highest levels of the Nazi Party and government at a conference in Wannsee, a suburb of Berlin. That solution was genocide—an attempt to wipe out the entire Jewish population. It would come to be known as the Holocaust.

After World War II began, the Nazis forced Jews to live in designated areas of a city, called ghettos. Jewish people lived in miserable conditions, isolated from the non-Jewish community. The Germans established more than 1,000 ghettos in Central and Eastern Europe. About 400,000 people were crowded into the Warsaw ghetto in Poland alone. Concentrating Jewish people in ghettos made it easier for the Nazis to round them up and send them to concentration camps.

In July 1944 Majdanek in Poland was the first death camp liberated by Soviet troops. Andrew Werth, a correspondent for *The Times of London* and the British Broadcasting Corporation (BBC), toured the camp one month after the liberation. His bosses at the BBC refused to air his report, though. The horrors that Werth reported were so shocking that they thought his story was based

A sign at one of the entrances to a ghetto in Lodz, Poland, warned: "Jewish area: entrance forbidden." Lodz became the second-largest ghetto created by the Nazis in Poland.

on Soviet propaganda. It was not until more camps were liberated that people began to understand and believe what had been happening.

THE DEATH CAMPS

When the Nazis invaded Poland in September 1939, they suddenly had millions more Jews in their control. Forcing Polish Jews and other people to emigrate wasn't going to work any better than it had in Germany. Instead, the Nazis decided to kill them.

The first wave of killings was carried out by special execution squads that followed the regular German army into Poland—as well as local people willing to cooperate with the Germans. The main targets were male Jews, Roman Catholic priests, Communists, and members of the wealthy or intellectual classes.

The execution squads rounded up their victims, took them to the outskirts of town, and forced them to dig mass graves. Then they lined their victims up on the edge of the graves and mowed them down with machine guns. Before the end of the war, women and children would be among the victims of the execution squads.

As the Germans advanced on the Soviet Union, millions more Jews came under their control. Nazi leaders came up with a new execution method for the Jews. They were placed in vans designed to allow the vehicles' exhaust to blow into the vans. The people inside died of carbon monoxide poisoning within 15 minutes.

Before long, the Nazis realized that the methods of killing Jews were too slow. Hitler and his

Deported Jewish people arrived at Auschwitz death camp in Poland. Auschwitz-Birkenau was the largest of the German concentration and extermination camps. Over 1 million Jewish people are thought to have died there, most of them in the gas chambers.

advisers decided that all the Jews of Europe were to be murdered—the Final Solution. The Nazis came up with the plan in January 1942 to expand some of their concentration camps into extermination camps.

The Germans and their allies in Europe rounded up Jews anywhere they could find them and sent them to extermination camps, which were equipped with gas chambers. Other prisoners were shot, beaten to death, or hanged. Thousands more died from the deadly infectious diseases such as typhoid fever, malaria, and tuberculosis that swept through the camps. Still others starved to death. The Nazis murdered 6 million Jews, two-thirds of the Jews living in Europe in 1939.

Although most people did not know what was going on inside the camps, Allied leaders did. The only solution they could find to ending the genocide, though, was to defeat Germany as quickly as possible. They believed that winning the war was the only way to end the Holocaust.

A storeroom held the clothes of murdered prisoners.

The war in Europe ended in April 1945, but Hitler never paid for his crimes. He shot himself April 30, 1945, as the Soviet army advanced on his bunker in Berlin. The next day Goebbels and his wife poisoned their six children before committing suicide. But the war continued in the Pacific until after the Allies dropped atomic bombs on the cities of Hiroshima and Nagasaki in early August 1945. Japan agreed to surrender August 14, and the war formally ended in September with an Allied victory.

Once again, Germany was brought to its knees after a world war that it had largely caused. The country split into two after the war ended. East Germany was under the Soviet Union's control and had a communist government, and West Germany was a democracy. East and West Germany were united into one Germany on October 3, 1990. Today the unified Germany is a democracy and is a strong ally of the United States and other western nations.

PUNISHING WAR CRIMINALS

In 1945, after the war ended, a special court was created to bring to trial the top Nazi officials responsible for the Holocaust. The International Military Tribunal at Nuremberg convened in November, and the trials continued until October 1, 1946. The court indicted 24 people and six Nazi organizations, including the Gestapo. During the trials much of the evidence about the planning of

Military police kept a close eye on Nazi officials during war crimes trials in Nuremberg.

Kristallnacht became public. Twelve of the defendants at Nuremberg were condemned to death, including Hermann Göring. He killed himself with a cyanide pill October 15, 1946, the day before he was scheduled to be hanged.

And what became of Herschel Grynszpan? He was never tried for his crime. The French government was afraid to stage a trial. If a jury found Grynszpan not guilty, the Nazis would retaliate against France. When Germany invaded France, Grynszpan was transferred to the Sachsenhausen concentration camp. The Nazis intended to use Grynszpan's trial as a propaganda tool, so he received good care in prison. They were never able to make the trial happen on their terms, though. Grynszpan spent most of the war at Sachsenhausen. But by 1942 his name disappeared from German record books. No one knows for sure what happened to him, but it's widely believed that he died in the camp.

His family, for the most part, was much more fortunate. His parents and siblings were able to escape Poland during the German invasion. They settled in the Soviet Union and moved to Israel after the war. His uncle Abraham, however, died in Auschwitz.

TIMELINE

▶ **November 11, 1918**
World War I
officially ends

▶ **November 8–9, 1923**
Adolf Hitler leads a
failed Nazi attempt to
take over the German
government known as
the Beer Hall Putsch

▶ **September 15, 1935**
Nuremberg Laws
are enacted

▶ **March 13, 1938**
Anschluss, the
annexation of
Austria, occurs

▶ **April 26, 1938**
New rule requires
declaration of all Jewish
property valued at more
than 5,000 reichsmarks

▶ **June 9, 1938**
Main synagogue in
Munich is torn down
and a parking lot built
in its place

▶ **July 6–15, 1938**
International conference
to discuss the issue of
Jewish refugees takes
place in Evian, France

▶ **August 17, 1938**
Decree is issued
requiring Jews to add the
names Israel and Sarah

▶ **November 9, 1938**
Vom Rath dies; Joseph
Goebbels gives a speech
during a Nazi gathering
and blames all Jews for
vom Rath's death

▶ **October 5, 1938**
Jewish passports are
no longer valid; identity
cards are required

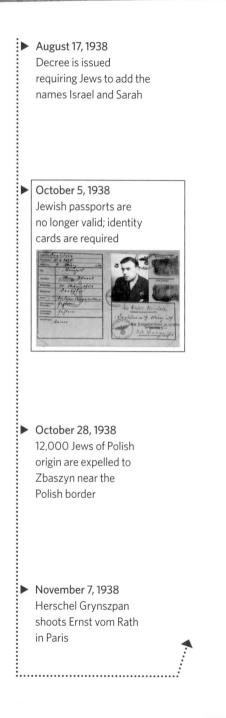

▶ **November 9–10, 1938**
Jewish businesses,
homes, and synagogues
are attacked during
Kristallnacht

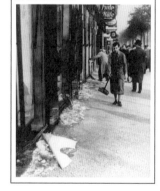

▶ **October 28, 1938**
12,000 Jews of Polish
origin are expelled to
Zbaszyn near the
Polish border

▶ **November 7, 1938**
Herschel Grynszpan
shoots Ernst vom Rath
in Paris

▶ **November 11, 1938**
Goebbels holds a press
conference for foreign
correspondents and
blames German citizens
for Kristallnacht

November 12, 1938
Decree is issued demanding "atonement payments" from German Jews for Kristallnacht damages

December 3, 1938
The Decree on the Utilization of Jewish Property forces Jewish business owners to sell their property to non-Jews; they receive a fraction of its value

November 14, 1938
Jews are forbidden to attend cultural events

December 6, 1938
Jews are forbidden to drive or walk in certain places

November 15, 1938
Jewish children are banned from German public schools; U.S. President Franklin D. Roosevelt publicly condemns the Nazi actions during Kristallnacht

September 1, 1939
Germany invades Poland; two days later, Great Britain and France declare war on Germany; World War II begins

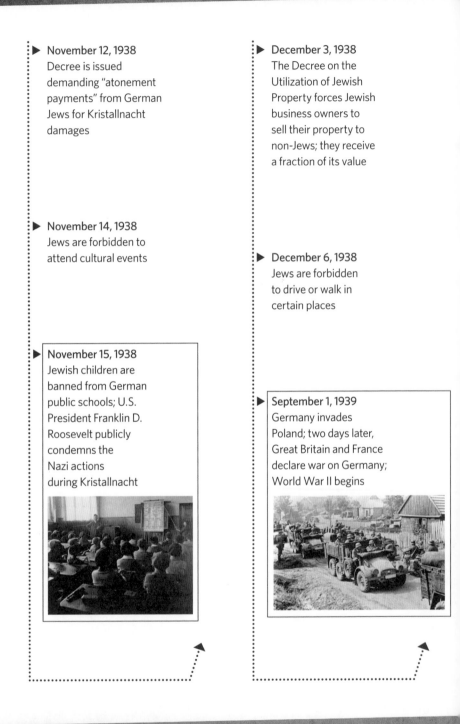

▶ **July 1944**
Soviet soldiers liberate
the death camp
Majdanek in Poland

▶ **April 30, 1945**
Hitler commits suicide
in his bunker; Joseph
Goebbels commits
suicide the next day

▶ **May 8, 1945**
Germany surrenders to
the Allies; the war ends
in Europe

▶ **August 14, 1945**
Japan's Emperor
Hirohito agrees to
surrender to the Allies;
the war officially ends in
September

GLOSSARY

allies—friends or helpers; when capitalized, refers to the United States and its allies during major wars

anti-Semitism—prejudice or discrimination against Jewish people

Aryan—term used by Nazis to describe a supposed master race of pureblooded Germans with blond hair and blue eyes

assassination—murder of someone who is well known or important, often for political reasons

bar mitzvah—ceremony and celebration that takes place on or near a Jewish boy's 13th birthday; girls have a similar ceremony called a bat mitzvah

chancellor—the head of government in some countries, such as Germany

communism—system in which goods and property are owned by the government and shared in common; communist rulers limit personal freedoms to achieve their goals

concentration camps—prison camps where thousands of inmates are held under harsh conditions

coup—sudden change of government, often by force

democracy—form of government in which the people elect their leaders

dictator—ruler who takes complete control of a country, often unjustly

discrimination—unfair treatment of a person or group, often because of race, religion, gender, sexual preference, or age

emigrate—to leave a home country to settle in another country permanently

fascism—government system that promotes extreme nationalism, repression, and anticommunism, and is ruled by a dictator

führer—German word meaning "leader"

indict—to charge with a crime

kosher—prepared according to Jewish dietary laws

paranoia—irrational or unfounded feelings of mistrust and suspicion

parliament—in some countries, a group of people elected to make laws

pogrom—organized attack on a minority group, especially Jews

putsch—violent attempt to overthrow a government

swastika—cross with bent arms that the Nazi Party used as its symbol

synagogue—Jewish place of worship

FURTHER READING

Berne, Emma Carlson. *Escaping the Nazis on the Kindertransport.* North Mankato, Minn.: Capstone Press, 2017.

Byers, Ann. *Kristallnacht and Living in Nazi Germany.* New York: Rosen Publishing, 2015.

Freeburg, Jessica. *Fight for Survival: The Story of the Holocaust.* North Mankato, Minn.: Capstone Press, 2017.

Langley, Andrew. *Hitler and Kristallnacht.* Chicago: Heinemann Library, 2014.

INTERNET SITES

Use FactHound to find Internet sites related to this book.

Visit *www.facthound.com*
Just type in 9780756555832 and go.

CRITICAL THINKING QUESTIONS

Germany's leaders felt that the rest of the world had treated the country unfairly after World War I. Do you think this treatment justified their actions after the war? Why or why not? Support your answer with evidence from the text.

Most non-Jewish people in Germany and Austria didn't try to help their Jewish neighbors during Kristallnacht for fear that they would also be punished. What do you think about their lack of action? Would you have done things differently in the same situation?

Before and during World War II, Jewish people were discriminated against by various governments. Why do you think people today still face discrimination because of race, religion, or other factors?

SOURCE NOTES

Page 7, line 9: Mitchell G. Bard. *48 Hours of Kristallnacht Night of Destruction/Dawn of the Holocaust: An Oral History.* Guilford, Conn.: Lyons Press, 2008, pp. 60–61.

Page 10, line 9: Ibid., p. 62.

Page 11, line 2: "German mobs' vengeance on Jews—Nov. 11, 1938." *The Telegraph.* 11 Nov. 2008. 21 Dec. 2016. http://www.telegraph.co.uk/history/britain-at-war/3418286/German-mobs-vengence-on-Jews-Nov-11-1938.html

Page 19, line 4 "The German Hyperinflation, 1923." Commanding Heights: The Battle for the World Economy. PBS. 21 Dec. 2016. https://www.pbs.org/wgbh/commandingheights/shared/minitext/ess_germanhyperinflation.html

Page 31, col. 2, line 1: Marion A. Kaplan. *Between Dignity and Despair: Jewish Life in Nazi Germany.* New York: Oxford University Press, 1998, pp. 33–34.

Page 36, col. 2, line 2: "The Rise of Adolf Hitler." The History Place. 27 Dec. 2016. http://www.historyplace.com/worldwar2/riseofhitler/father.htm

Page 43, col. 2, line 2: *Between Dignity and Despair: Jewish Life in Nazi Germany,* p. 35.

Page 44, line 3: Anthony Read and David Fisher. *Kristallnacht: The Nazi Night of Terror.* New York: Times Books, 1989, p. 28.

Page 51, col. 2, line 2: "Chronology of Jewish Persecution: 1933." Jewish Virtual Library. 27 Dec. 2016. http://www.jewishvirtuallibrary.org/timeline-of-jewish-persecution-in-the-holocaust

Page 53, line 5: *Kristallnacht: The Nazi Night of Terror,* p. 30.

Page 58, line 18: Jonathan Kirsch. *The Short, Strange Life of Herschel Grynszpan: A Boy Avenger, a Nazi Diplomat, and a Murder in Paris.* New York: Liveright Publishing Corporation, 2013, p. 83.

Page 60, line 16: *Kristallnacht: The Nazi Night of Terror,* p. 48.

Page 62, line 8: Ibid., p. 51.

Page 64, line 1: *The Short, Strange Life of Herschel Grynszpan: A Boy Avenger, a Nazi Diplomat, and a Murder in Paris,* pp. 108–109

Page 64, line 16: *Kristallnacht: The Nazi Night of Terror,* p. 8.

Page 65, col. 1, line 8: Ibid., p. 51.

Page 68, line 5: Ibid., p. 61.

Page 68, line 21: Volker Ullrich. *Hitler: Ascent, 1889–1939.* New York: Alfred A. Knopf, 2016, p. 669.

Page 69, line 9: *Kristallnacht: The Nazi Night of Terror,* p. 62.

Page 69, line 18: Anthony Read. *The Devil's Disciples: Hitler's Inner Circle.* New York: W. W. Norton, 2004, p. 510.

Page 75, col. 1, line 10: Rabbi Marvin Hier. "Kristallnacht Seventy Years Later—'Was There No Space in the World for Us?'" 2008. 28 Dec. 2016. Simon Wiesenthal Center. http://www.wiesenthal.com/site/apps/nlnet/content2.aspx?c=lsKWLbPJLnF&b=4924937&ct=6346483

Page 77, line 1: Lyn Smith. *Remembering: Voices of the Holocaust: A New History in the Words of the Men and Women Who Survived.* New York: Carroll & Graf, 2006, p. 50.

Page 77, line 20: Martin Gilbert. *Kristallnacht: Prelude to Destruction.* New York: HarperCollins, 2006, pp. 80–81.

Page 82, col. 1, line 9: *Kristallnacht: The Nazi Night of Terror,* p. 166.

Page 86, line 4: Ibid., p. 162.

Page 88, line 2: Rafael Medoff. "Kristallnacht—and the World's Response." November 2003. 28 Dec. 2016. The David S. Wyman Institute for Holocaust Studies. http://www.wymaninstitute.org/articles/2003-11-kristalln.php

Page 88, line 6: Arthur Sears Henning. "President Rips into Nazis for Harassing Jews." *The Daily Chicago Tribune.* 16 Nov. 1938, p. 3. 28 Dec. 2016. http://archives.chicagotribune.com/1938/11/16/page/3/article/president-rips-into-nazis-for-harassing-jews

SELECT BIBLIOGRAPHY

"Adolf Hitler." History. 29 Dec. 2016. http://www.history.com/topics/world-war-ii/adolf-hitler

Bard, Mitchell G. *48 Hours of Kristallnacht Night of Destruction/Dawn of the Holocaust: An Oral History*. Guilford, Conn.: Lyons Press, 2008.

"Commanding Heights: The Battle for the World Economy." 21 April 2017. PBS. http://www.pbs.org/wgbh/commandingheights/

Gilbert, Martin. *Kristallnacht: Prelude to Destruction*. New York: HarperCollins, 2006.

Henning, Arthur Sears. "President Rips into Nazis for Harassing Jews." *The Daily Chicago Tribune*. 16 Nov. 1938, p. 3. 28 Dec. 2016. http://archives.chicagotribune.com/1938/11/16/page/3/article/president-rips-into-nazis-for-harassing-jews

Hier, Marvin. "Kristallnacht Seventy Years Later—'Was There No Space in the World for Us?'" 2008. 28 Dec. 2016. Simon Wiesenthal Center. http://www.wiesenthal.com/site/apps/nlnet/content2.aspx?c=lsKWLbPJLnF&b=4924937&ct=6346483

Holocaust Education & Archive Research Team. 29 Dec. 2016. http://www.holocaustresearchproject.org/toc.html

Jewish Virtual Library. 29 Dec. 2016. http://www.jewishvirtuallibrary.org

Kaplan, Marion A. *Between Dignity and Despair: Jewish Life in Nazi Germany*. New York: Oxford University Press, 1998.

Kirsch, Jonathan. *The Short, Strange Life of Herschel Grynszpan: A Boy Avenger, a Nazi Diplomat, and a Murder in Paris*. New York: Liveright Publishing Corporation, 2013.

Laqueur, Walter. *Generation Exodus: The Fate of Young Jewish Refugees from Nazi Germany*. Hanover, N.H.: Brandeis University Press, 2001.

Medoff, Rafael. "Kristallnacht—and the World's Response." November 2003. 28 Dec. 2016. The David S. Wyman Institute for Holocaust Studies. http://www.wymaninstitute.org/articles/2003-11-kristalln.php

Read, Anthony. *The Devil's Disciples: Hitler's Inner Circle*. New York: W. W. Norton, 2004.

Read, Anthony, and David Fisher. *Kristallnacht: The Nazi Night of Terror*. New York: Times Books, 1989.

"The Rise of Adolf Hitler." The History Place. 29 Dec. 2016. http://www.historyplace.com/worldwar2/riseofhitler/index.htm

Schwab, Gerald. *The Day the Holocaust Began: The Odyssey of Herschel Grynszpan*. New York: Praeger, 1990.

Smith, Lyn. *Remembering: Voices of the Holocaust: A New History in the Words of the Men and Women Who Survived*. New York: Carroll & Graf, 2006.

Ullrich, Volker. *Hitler: Ascent, 1889–1939*. New York: Alfred A. Knopf, 2016.

United States Holocaust Memorial Museum. 29 Dec. 2016. https://www.ushmm.org

INDEX